# Uranus

## by
## Christine Taylor-Butler

Children's Press
An Imprint of Scholastic Inc.
New York  Toronto  London  Auckland  Sydney
Mexico City  New Delhi  Hong Kong
Danbury, Connecticut

These content vocabulary word builders
are for grades 1–2.

Consultant: Michelle Yehling, Astronomy Education Consultant

Photo Credits:

Photographs © 2008: AP/Wide World Photos: cover; Getty Images/Antonio M. Rosario: 9; NASA: 4 bottom right, 5 top left, 15, 17 (JPL), back cover, 1, 2, 4 top, 5 bottom, 7, 13, 14, 19, 23 right; Photo Researchers, NY/Detlev van Ravenswaay: 4 bottom left; PhotoDisc/via SODA: 23 left.

Illustration Credits:

Diagram on pages 20–21 by Greg Harris          Illustration on page 5 and 11 by Pat Rasch

Book Design: Simonsays Design!
Book Production: The Design Lab

Library of Congress Cataloging-in-Publication Data
Taylor-Butler, Christine.
Uranus / by Christine Taylor-Butler.—Updated ed.
    p. cm.—(Scholastic news nonfiction readers)
Includes bibliographical references and index.
ISBN-13: 978-0-531-14754-2 (lib. bdg.)          978-0-531-14769-6 (pbk.)
ISBN-10: 0-531-14754-1 (lib. bdg.)          0-531-14769-X (pbk.)
1. Uranus (Planet)—Juvenile literature. I. Title.
QB681.T39 2007
523.47—dc22          2006102777

1 2 3 4 5 6 7 8 9 10 R   17 16 15 14 13 12 11 10 09 08

# CONTENTS

# WORD HUNT

Look for these words as you read. They will be in **bold**.

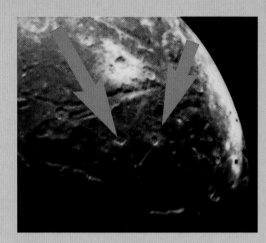

**craters**
(**kray**-turz)

**solar system**
(**soh**-lur **siss**-tuhm)

**Titania**
(tuh-**tane**-yuh)

4

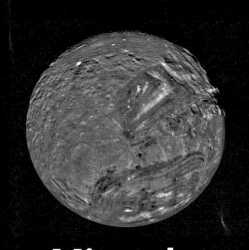

# Miranda
(muh-**ran**-duh)

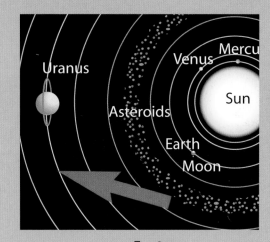

Uranus

Venus

Mercu

Asteroids

Sun

Earth

Moon

# orbit
(**or**-bit)

# Uranus
(**yur**-uh-nus)

# *Voyager 2*
(**voi**-ij-uhr 2)

# Uranus!

**Uranus** has clouds of gas. The gas is very cold.

Closer to the planet the gas turns into icy slush.

7

Uranus is the seventh planet from the Sun.

Uranus is one of the biggest planets in our **solar system**.

Sun

Uranus

9

Uranus travels around the Sun on a path called an **orbit**.

Most planets also spin like tops along their orbits. But Uranus spins like a ball rolling.

Scientists think Uranus was hit by something that tipped it sideways.

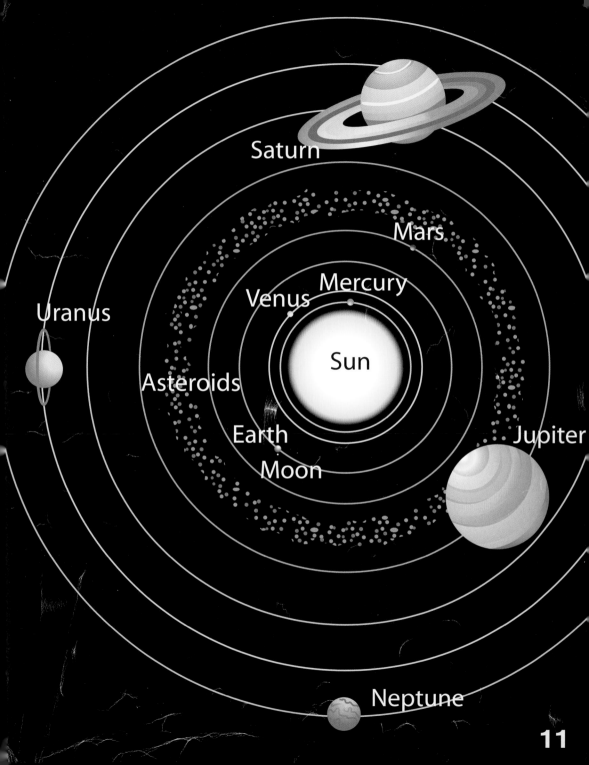

Saturn

Mars

Mercury

Venus

Uranus

Sun

Asteroids

Earth

Moon

Jupiter

Neptune

Uranus has 11 rings.

They are hard to see.

The rings on Uranus are made of ice. The ice is covered in dark dust.

13

Uranus has at least 27 moons.

The largest moon is **Titania**.

Titania has **craters**, like Earth's moon.

It also has long, deep marks that stretch around it.

crater

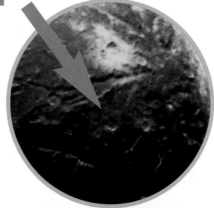

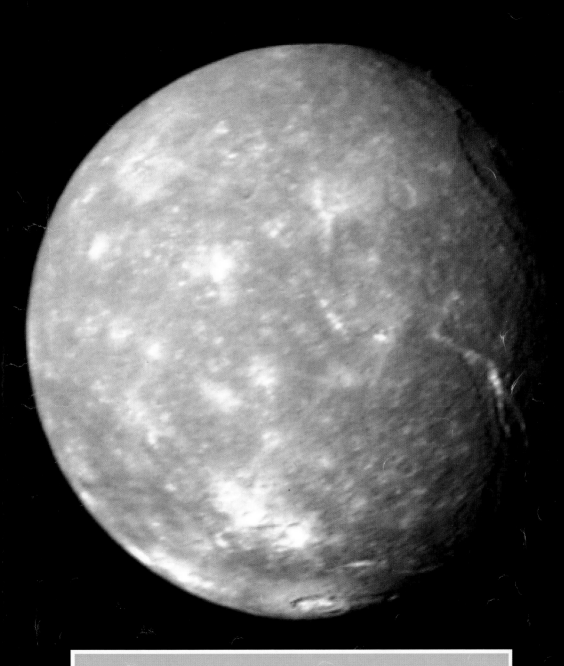

**Titania was first seen in 1787.**

**Miranda** is also one of Uranus's moons.

Miranda is one of the oddest worlds anywhere.

It has craters. It has long marks. It has broken rocks. It has giant cliffs.

Scientists know how Miranda got some marks, but they do not know about them all.

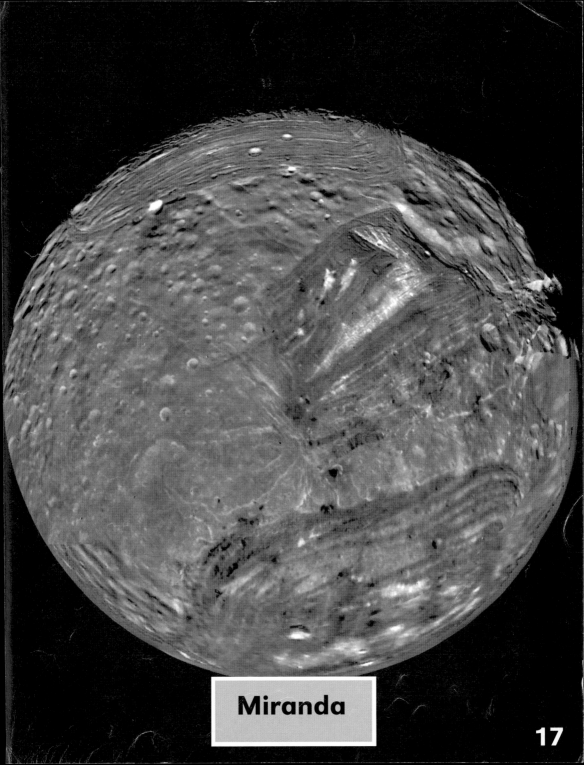

**Miranda**

***Voyager 2*** is a space probe.

It is the only craft to go near Uranus.

It is why we know more about this planet.

Thank you, *Voyager 2*!

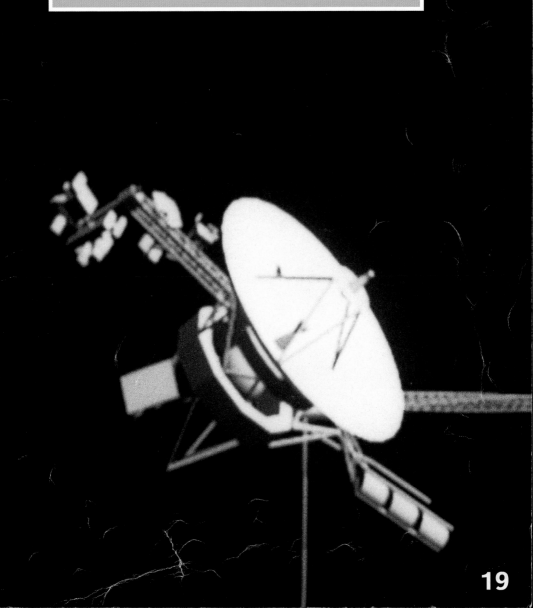

*Voyager 2* first went into space in 1977.

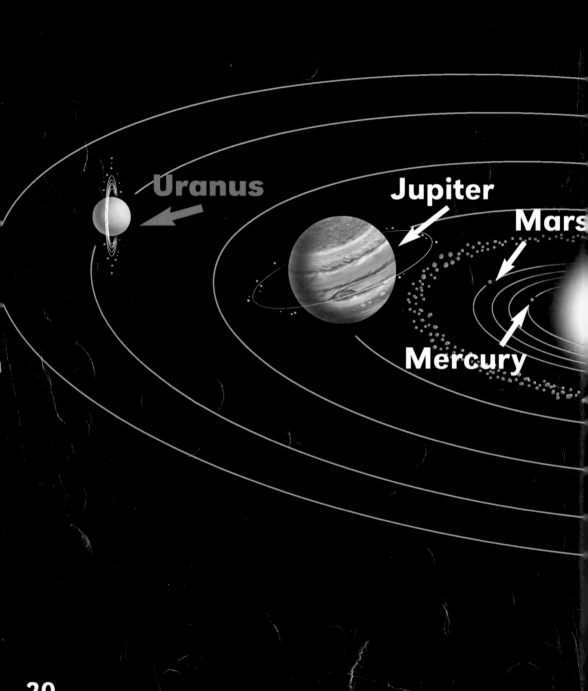

Uranus

Jupiter

Mars

Mercury

# URANUS

## IN OUR SOLAR SYSTEM

Saturn

Sun

Venus

Earth

Neptune

# YOUR NEW WORDS

**craters** (**kray**-turz) large dents or holes in an object

**Miranda** (muh-**ran**-duh) one of Uranus's moons

**orbit** (**or**-bit) the path an object takes around another object

**solar system** (**soh**-lur **siss**-tuhm) the group of planets, moons, and other things that travel around the Sun

**Titania** (tuh-**tane**-yuh) Uranus's largest moon

**Uranus** (**yur**-uh-nus) a planet named after the Greek god of the sky

***Voyager 2*** (**voi**-ij-uhr 2) the first and only space probe to visit Uranus and Neptune

# Earth and Uranus

A year is how long it takes a planet to go around the Sun.

 **1 Earth year =365 days**

 **1 Uranus year =30,687 Earth days**

A day is how long it takes a planet turn one time.

 **1 Earth day = 24 hours**

 **1 Uranus day = 17 Earth hours**

A moon is an object that circles around a planet.

 **Earth has 1 moon.**

 **Uranus has at least 27 moons with more being found all the time.**

**Scientists do not agree on which way is North on Uranus.**

# INDEX

## FIND OUT MORE

### Book:

Burnham, Robert. *Children's Atlas of the Universe*. Pleasantville, NY: Reader's Digest Children's Publishing, Inc., 2000.

### Web site:

Solar System Exploration
*http://sse.jpl.nasa.gov/planets*

## MEET THE AUTHOR

**Christine Taylor-Butler** is the author of more than twenty books for children. She holds a degree in Engineering from M.I.T. She lives in Kansas City with her family, where they have a telescope for searching the skies.